PUFFINS

WITHDRAWN

Wildlife Monographs – Puffins
Copyright © 2007 Evans Mitchell Books

Text and Photography Copyright © 2007 Heather Angel
Reprinted in 2008, and 2012

Heather Angel has asserted her rights to be identified
as the author and photographer of this work in
accordance with Section 77 of the Copyright,
Designs and Patents Act 1988.

First published in the United Kingdom in 2007 by:
Evans Mitchell Books
86 Gloucester Place
London W1U 6HP
United Kingdom
www.embooks.co.uk

Design by:
Roy Platten
Eclipse
roy.eclipse@btopenworld.com

All rights reserved. No part of this publication may be
reproduced, stored in a retrieval system or transmitted in
any form or by any means; electronic, mechanical,
photocopying or otherwise, without the prior
written consent of the publisher.

British Library Cataloguing in Publication Data.
A CIP record of this book is available
on request from the British Library.

ISBN: 978-1-901268-19-5

Pre Press: F E Burman, London, United Kingdom

Printed in China

PUFFINS

HIGHLAND
LIBRARIES

HEATHER ANGEL

Evans Mitchell Books

Contents

Left: A pair of puffins relax atop their breeding cliff in Iceland.

Introduction

Everyone loves puffins; indeed, their comical faces have earned them the alternative names of sea parrots and clowns of the sea. Watching puffins on cliff tops bedecked with flowers on a sunny day is idyllic; yet these sites – often rugged and remote – are far from idyllic when lashed by wind and rain.

Wildlife Monographs – Puffins reveals how these charismatic seabirds live and survive in a marine environment, which can be quite harsh in the winter. We see puffins in spring and summer on their breeding cliffs, but for the rest of the year they have to survive out in the open ocean. Puffins are not the most gainly as they walk on land, but once airborne they wheel and turn with great agility and their wings are also used to 'fly' underwater in pursuit of their fish prey.

Above: An Atlantic puffin *(Fratercula arctica)* looks around on a rocky outcrop in Lunga, Treshnish Isles, Scotland.

Right: A pair of Atlantic puffins hunkers down on a cliff top during a windy day in Iceland.

A boat trip past puffin cliffs will find birds rafting on the sea surface or flying to and from their feeding grounds. At the end of the day, after a hard day's fishing, puffins tend to gather outside their burrows; but to fully appreciate their way of life, you need to spend time on land throughout the day. The images here portray the comings and goings of puffins during the time they are breeding on land. There are puffins courting, collecting nesting material, flying off to feed and returning with fish, preening, flapping their wings and snoozing.

Left: A puffin lowers its feet as it comes in to land.

Right: At the end of a day's fishing puffins gather on a rocky outcrop on Grimsey Island, Iceland.

Below: Apart from the puffins themselves, one of the delights of visiting a puffinry in summer is the swards of wildflowers that enliven many cliff tops.

To understand the broader picture of the factors that are now impinging on Atlantic puffin populations, we have to turn to the work of field biologists. In recent years, overfishing for sandeels and climate change have both had an impact on puffins. Rising seawater temperatures have impacted both on the food and the breeding time of the sandeel – the puffin's favoured food when breeding. This has resulted in puffin chicks literally starving to death. Up-to-date research has revealed the drama which is unfolding in the North Sea.

Iceland is the Atlantic puffin capital, where some sixty percent of the world population returns to breed. Puffins are still caught here for food and each year on Heimaey, in the Westmann Islands, children rescue puffin fledglings that end up in town, disorientated by street lights at night, so they can release them into the air the next day.

Left: Puffins outside their burrows on Látrabjarg cliffs, Iceland.

History and distribution

People living on remote offshore islands where puffins breed have for long been dependent on these birds as a source of food. Indeed, the agile way a puffin swims underwater led people to assume it was a cross between a bird and a fish. This belief permitted some people to eat puffin meat during Lent and on Fridays when meat was prohibited by the Catholic church.

Puffins, together with guillemots (or murres), auklets and the razorbill, are gregarious seabirds that belong to the auk family. There are four kinds of puffins, although only three species are called puffins – the Atlantic, tufted, and horned; the fourth is known as the rhinoceros auklet. All four species are confined to the Northern Hemisphere oceans. Most of this book relates to the Atlantic puffin, with some comparisons made with other puffins.

Opposite page: A turf-covered cliff top on an offshore island, such as here on one of the Westmann Islands off south Iceland, is the favoured breeding terrain of Atlantic puffins, which frequent the northern Atlantic Ocean.

Above: An Atlantic puffin pauses on a cliff top ledge at Látrabjarg in Iceland.

None of the 23 species of auks match the size of the great auk or garefowl *(Pinguinus impennis)* that became extinct in the mid-nineteenth century. This flightless auk had a massive bill as well as large black webbed feet with claws, and reached some 75 centimetres tall, almost twice as high as its nearest relative, the razorbill. The great auk's atrophied wings were used solely for underwater flight. Indeed, this highly specialised fish eater was adept at chasing its prey underwater.

Being a strong swimmer, the great auk would overwinter as far south as Spain and Florida. But on land, its clumsy upright gait was no match for the local inhabitants of North America and Europe. Unlike other auks, great auks could not escape by flying out to sea, so once cornered they were doomed. During the eighteenth century large numbers were herded into pens and clubbed to death. Starving sailors welcomed great auks as a source of fresh meat after a long sea voyage, while feather merchants used feathers to stuff pillows and cushions as well as for decorating hats.

By the early part of the nineteenth century the last stronghold of the great auk was the Icelandic island of Geirfuglasker. The topography made it impossible for sailors to gain a landing, but when it was destroyed by a submarine eruption in 1830 the surviving auks transferred to Eldey Island. Here, unless

Above: The great auk *(Pinguinuis imperris)* was a huge flightless bird almost twice the height of a razorbill. This watercolour by William MacGillivray shows the massive bill and small wings. *Photo: Natural History Museum, London.*

Opposite page: An Atlantic puffin looks out to sea from Heimaey with another of the Westmann Islands in the distance, Iceland.

the weather was very rough, a landing was possible. Once the new great auk site was discovered, each time the island was raided during the period 1830-1844 fewer and fewer auks were bagged, until in June 1844 the last two great auks were collected from Eldey. Today, all that remains of the great auk are stuffed specimens, and eggs scattered in museums around the world. In 1971 the Director of the Icelandic Natural History Museum paid the equivalent of 9,000 pounds sterling for the mounted skin of a great auk. Bones of great auks have been found in Norwegian kitchen middens dating back some several thousand years. Over-collection during the breeding season certainly exacerbated the demise of the great auk, but it is possible that environmental changes were also a contributing factor.

Long before sailors ventured into southern waters and found many more flightless birds adopting a similar upright stance to the great auk, they referred to it as a penguin. Once the great auk became extinct, the original name – thought by some to be derived from the Welsh words *pen* (head) and *gwyn* (white), possibly referring to a large white patch between each eye and the bill – was no longer used.

Puffins have for long been collected by man for food, but because their distribution is much broader and their numbers much larger than the great auk, they have never been threatened. However, the greatest threat to puffins today may be the increase in sea temperature brought about by climate change.

Puffins spend most of the year out at sea, and only come ashore to breed, typically on remote offshore – often uninhabited – islands, although some puffin colonies occur on the mainland.

As the name suggests, the realm of the Atlantic puffin *(Fratercula arctica)* is the Atlantic Ocean; breeding on both the eastern and western coasts, as far south as Maine in the United States (44°N) and as far north as the high Arctic in Svalbard (78°N). This is the smallest of the three puffins, reaching some 30 centimetres high. When detailed research work has been carried out in a puffin colony over a period of many years, it is possible to see upward or downward trends. For instance, work by Dr Mike Harris on puffin populations on St Kilda – off the north west of Scotland – has shown they have declined during the latter part of the twentieth century, whereas on the Isle of May in the Firth of Forth, puffins have made a spectacular increase.

Above: The tufted puffin *(Fratercula cirrhata)* breeds in the northern part of the Pacific Ocean and is the largest of all the puffins.

Opposite page: An Atlantic puffin flies past a cliff top in Iceland.

Because many puffin breeding sites are on remote inaccessible islands, it is much more difficult to be precise about the world population of each species. None the less, it is thought that the total Atlantic puffin population is in the region of 7 million pairs, with almost half of them occurring in Iceland (both on the mainland and offshore islands).

Biologists distinguish three distinct subspecies of Atlantic puffins based on body size. The most widespread and also the most abundant is *Fratercula arctica arctica*, which breeds on the north American coast from Maine to Newfoundland in Canada, on Baffin Island, in east Greenland, Iceland and Norway. Smaller in size, *Fratercula arctica grabae* returns to the Faroe Islands, Britain, Ireland and France to breed. The largest subspecies of Atlantic puffin – *Fratercula arctica naumanni* – is also the rarest and can be found on Svalbard and north east Greenland.

Tufted and horned puffins both frequent the northern part of the Pacific Ocean, where they spend most of the year. Tufted puffins *(Fratercula cirrhata)* share some of their breeding range with horned puffins, but they breed further south – down as far as the Channel Islands in lower California, where they nest amongst cacti. Their range spans over 35° latitude, up via the Oregon, Washington and British Columbia coasts to the Gulf of Alaska, the Aleutian Islands and across the Pacific to northern Japan and the Russian Far East, including the Sea of Okhotsk, the Kurils, the Bering and Chukchi Seas. Come the winter, tufted puffins head south from their breeding grounds, not least because the Bering, Chukchi and Okhotsk Seas become iced up.

Horned puffins *(Fratercula corniculata)* on the other hand, breed only as far south as British Columbia in Canada, but extend further north than tufted puffins, breeding on the northern Alaskan coast, the Aleutian Islands and across the sea along the eastern Siberian coastline. The biggest concentration – some 370,000 birds – breed on the Semidi Islands in the Gulf of Alaska. The Semidi Islands Wildlife Refuge also attracts several other auks, notably murres (one million plus), ancient murrelets and parakeet auklets, to breed there. Even so, the seabird populations are kept in check by populations of arctic foxes originating from animals released by fox farmers in the 1880s.

Distinguishing features

Puffins are all stocky seabirds that congregate at their breeding sites for a few brief months each summer. Only at this time of year can we appreciate the colourful breeding dress of these clowns of the sea.

The smallest puffin of the trio is the Atlantic puffin, which breeds both in Europe and on the Atlantic coast of North America. Standing on a cliff top, looking out to sea, the birds with their white chests and black backs resemble men waiting to dine in their dinner jackets. This countershading – also found on the horned puffin and penguins – helps the birds to blend in with the surroundings when swimming underwater. If viewed from below, their pale undersides merge in with the brighter sea above, thereby making them more difficult for underwater predators to spot from below; while the dark back viewed from above blends into the dark water below. Melanin pigments not only add colour to the dark feathers, but also make them denser and therefore more resistant to wear and tear as puffins enter and leave their burrows.

Opposite page: The tufted puffin has a massive orange bill with grooves that curve towards the tip. The golden head plumes are shown off to advantage against the all-black body.

Above: An Atlantic puffin in full breeding livery sports orange-red legs and feet and a stunning multi-coloured bill.

All puffins develop their breeding dress by growing colourful bill plates and enriching the colour of their legs and feet. The bright orange-red legs and feet of Atlantic puffins have well-developed black toenails for digging. Puffin bills are made of keratin (like our own fingernails and toenails) and are compressed sideways. In profile they appear wide, but are narrow when seen head-on. Both the upper and lower bill are blue-grey at the base, grading through yellow to a bright red tip.

Grooves or furrows in the bill provide a rough guide to the age of a puffin; two grooves indicate the bird is adult and has reached breeding age. But unlike tree rings, puffins do not then develop an extra groove for each successive year, so it becomes much more difficult to age older puffins precisely. The bill is used for digging, fighting, gathering food and for billing (when a pair knock their bills together to court and pair bond).

The upper part of the bill is neatly outlined by a yellow fleshy strip, known as a cere; beneath this is a yellow fleshy patch that expands to form the base of the gape when the bill is open. The eyes have dark centres with an outer red orbital ring and have blue patches of skin above and below. It is difficult to tell the difference between the sexes, although the male has a larger bill.

Opposite page: All puffins have webbed feet with long sharp toenails used to grip onto slippery surfaces and for digging out the burrow. The innermost toe curves inwards to prevent it becoming worn down by repeated landing on rocks.

Top: Only mature breeding Atlantic puffins sport the striking broad bill with a bluish base bounded by a yellow band and a bright red tip, seen here from the side. Notice the grooves curve towards the head.

Middle: When a puffin's head is viewed head-on, the extreme side-to-side flattening of the bill immediately becomes obvious.

Bottom: Each dark Atlantic puffin eye is encircled by a red ring set within the off-white feathers. Above and below the eye are dark cornified skin patches.

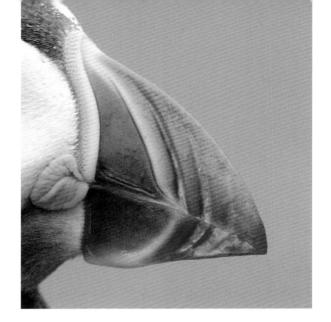

After the breeding season, the bright legs and feet fade to a dull yellow, the bill plates are shed as nine fragments, and the white face becomes darker. Adults in winter, as well as immature puffins, are not dissimilar (although immature birds have smaller and more pointed bills) and appear so different from the familiar gaudy breeding birds, it was once thought they were different species. Puffins become flightless for a while after the flight feathers moult.

Left: A puffin flexes its wings while ashore during a rainy day on Lunga, one of the Treshnish Isles. The relatively small wings beat up to 400 times a minute to propel the rotund seabird through the air, and function as paddles when it swims underwater.

Above: A tufted puffin flexes its wings whilst rafting on the water.

Unlike Atlantic and horned puffins, tufted puffins have black bodies, yellow-orange feet and legs, a massive triangular orange bill, a red orbital ring around the eye, and golden head plumes, which disappear after the breeding season. This largest puffin is a flamboyant auk, which resembles a dandy in gothic clothing with long golden locks.

Above: Back at the colony, puffins repeatedly preen their feathers to keep them in good condition, most often using their bill as here.

24

Like the Atlantic puffin, the horned puffin has a white chest; with the black neck strap above resembling a black choker. The large triangular, red-tipped yellow bill is translucent and glows when backlit by the sun. Even though the horned puffin shares the same ocean as the tufted puffin, it is quite distinct, with a white chest and yellow bill.

Left: Puffins preen both on land and on the water, as shown here by this tufted puffin at Living Coasts in Devon.

Below: On land, puffins are constantly on the alert, turning their head from one side to the other keeping a lookout for predators.

Puffins worldwide

Order: *Charadriformes*
Family: *Alcidae* (auklets, razorbill, guillemots or murres and puffins)

Puffins belong to the auk family, a group of 23 species of seabirds that are confined to the northern hemisphere and are adapted to fly, to swim underwater and to walk on land.

Within the Pacific Ocean there are 17 endemic species, including the tufted and horned puffins and the rhinoceros auklet, which is classed as a puffin. Only four species of auk are endemic to the Atlantic Ocean, including the Atlantic puffin. Two other species occur in both oceans.

Auks are highly gregarious seabirds that can congregate in huge numbers at their breeding colonies. Guillemots can form vast seabird 'cities' atop isolated rocky stacks, on sloping cliff ledges and on narrow horizontal ledges of vertical cliffs. Instead of building a nest, they lay their single egg directly on bare rock.

Little auks or dovekies breed in the Arctic, but may be seen as a winter visitor in British waters. This black and white bird has a small black bill and feeds on plankton as well as small fish.

Opposite page: Several other auks often share the same islands with breeding puffins. Guillemots *(Uria aalge)* have dark brown backs with white fronts and a narrow pointed bill. They lay their single egg directly on the cliff face and tend to crowd together.

Above: The little auk or dovekie *(Alle alle)* is a small auk half the size of the Atlantic puffin. It breeds on islands in the high Arctic within rock crevices. The tiny bill is used to catch crustaceans underwater,

27

Atlantic Puffin

Scientific name:	*Fratercula arctica*
World population:	circa 14 million birds
Height:	26-30cm
Weight:	320-480g
Incubation:	39-43 days
Hatching to fledging:	34-60 days
Adult food:	fish and pelagic marine invertebrates
Distribution:	Atlantic Ocean
Breeding areas:	northern Europe, Faroe Isles, Iceland, eastern North America

The Atlantic puffin has a white chest with a black back and when breeding it sports bright orange-red legs and feet, as well as a multicoloured bill. The bright red bill tip, which glows even in the drabbest of weathers, grades through yellow to a bluish base. The dark eyes are encircled by a red ring and have blue skin patches above and below each one.

This, the smallest puffin, breeds on both sides of the North Atlantic and seeks out soft peaty turf, which is easy for burrowing. Typical sites are grassy cliff tops or cliff ledges – often amongst coastal flowers, but on one site in Newfoundland puffins nest amongst trees. The largest colonies tend to be on uninhabited islands, or some way from human habitation. The chicks are fed largely on sandeels, which are carried by the adults crosswise in their bills – the record catch being 62 fish.

Once Atlantic puffins leave the breeding grounds, their red feet fade to a dull yellow and their eye-catching bills become drab and smaller in size as the outer plates are shed. Out in the open ocean Atlantic puffins feed not only on fish such as sandeels, saithe, whiting, capelin and herring but also on pelagic polychaete worms, shrimps and molluscs.

ATLANTIC OCEAN

Tufted Puffin

Scientific name:	*Fratercula cirrhata*
World population:	circa 3 million birds
Height or length:	40cm
Weight:	778-825g
Incubation:	43-46 days
Hatching to fledging:	47 days on average
Adult food:	fish and pelagic marine invertebrates
Distribution:	Northern Pacific Ocean
Breeding areas:	west coast North America, Aleutian Islands, north Japan, Russian Far East

When breeding, this largest puffin has an outsized triangular orange bill, white face mask, golden head plumes, yellow-orange feet and legs which contrast with the all-black body. Out of water, the golden head plumes curve behind the head, but as a tufted puffin swims underwater or flies into the wind, they stream behind it. The orbital ring of the eye changes from black to coral red in breeding birds when the iris is yellow or pale cream. At each corner of the mouth is a bright orange fleshy rosette.

Tufted puffins breed on both sides of the North Pacific, with 82 percent breeding in burrows excavated beneath the turf. Compared to horned puffins, they select a more diverse range of food for their single offspring, which includes a range of schooling fish, such as anchovy, capelin, lanternfish, young pollock and sandeels (sand lance). Predators of tufted puffins include bald eagles, peregrine falcons, snowy owls, arctic and red foxes as well as brown bears.

After breeding, the plumes disappear and the bill plates are shed to leave a smaller orange bill. Then, these puffins spend most of their time out in the ocean, where marine invertebrates – such as squid, polychaete worms and euphausiids – form a major part of their diet, which is supplemented by pelagic fish.

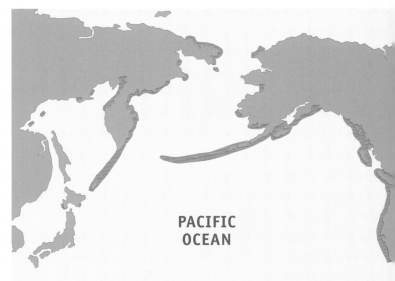

PACIFIC OCEAN

Horned Puffin

Scientific name: *Fratercula corniculata*
World population: circa 1 million birds
Height: 38cm
Weight: 483-648g
Incubation: 38-45 days
Hatching to fledging: 42 days on average
Adult food: fish and marine invertebrates
Distribution: northern Pacific Ocean
Breeding areas: west coast of North America, Semidi Islands, Aleutian Islands, Russian Far East

The horned puffin is slightly smaller than the tufted but larger than the Atlantic puffin. When breeding, it has a large triangular yellow bill with a red tip, plus an orange fleshy patch at the base of the gape. A dark fleshy strip extends vertically up from the eye giving the appearance of a horn – hence the common name. After breeding, the 'horn' is lost and the size of the bill reduced. The orbital ring of breeding birds is red and the iris light brown.

The distribution of the horned puffin overlaps with that of the tufted puffin, but it can easily be distinguished by the white chest, yellow bill and lack of feather plumes. Like the Atlantic puffin, it has a white chest but the two species cannot be confused since they reside in different oceans.

Horned puffins breed on exposed islands and mainland cliffs. Wherever possible, they select earthen burrows to rear their chicks, and it is here that the greatest density of birds is found, including the largest colony in Alaska. However, where the ground is hard they seek crevices in scree slopes or between boulders on beaches.

If land predators, such as arctic foxes, are present the puffins select crevices in rocky cliff faces.

Sandeels are the preferred food for their single chick. During the winter this pelagic species lives in central North Pacific oceanic waters, where some 70 percent of its diet is lanternfish, plus marine invertebrates including squid, polychaete worms and krill.

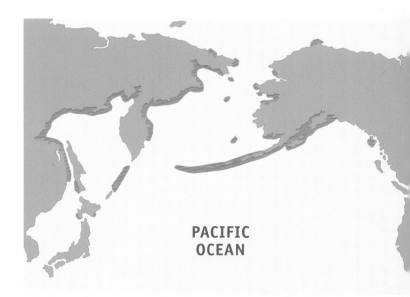

PACIFIC OCEAN

Habitat and diet

For almost two thirds of the year puffins live out at sea where they spend their time swimming, diving, feeding and rafting. They even roost at sea, with their bill tucked under a wing. The Atlantic puffin overwinters in the Atlantic ocean, the tufted and horned puffins in the North Pacific. Unlike other auks, puffins moult in late winter. After the wing and tail feathers have re-grown in spring, puffins begin to assemble offshore from where they left their burrows the previous summer. While the date of this return varies with latitude, the actual time is remarkably consistent – within a few days – for a given location.

The average date Atlantic puffins are seen off Skomer Island in south-west Wales is 23 March and they appear on land a week to ten days later. Further north, in the Faroes, they return on 14 April, the first day of summer, referred to by the local people as *summarmaladager*, which means return of the puffin. In Iceland, puffins come ashore at the end of April or even early May, while it is well into May before they come ashore in Greenland and Spitzbergen.

Opposite page: Puffins gather on a rock late in the day, Grimsey Island, Iceland.

Above: Sea mayweed is one of many maritime wildflowers that share the cliff top terrain with puffins in Iceland.

Puffins gather on the sea making short forays ashore, but if the weather deteriorates they tend to stay out at sea for slightly longer. If they fail to meet up with their mate at sea, they rendezvous at the burrow, then return to the sea to mate. The poor female is almost submerged by the weight of the male. A mating that takes place on land is rarely successful.

Atlantic puffins breed when they are five years old and keep the same mate for life and return to the same burrow from one year to the next. However, if no chicks are produced for several years, they will split up and find new mates. They breed in soft ground, preferably grass-covered peaty turf on small islands, on cliff tops, or vegetated cliff ledges facing the ocean. They prefer to nest near a cliff edge, but when these sites are occupied they will excavate burrows further inland. Puffins must surely have the prime real estate of any seabirds where their burrows are sited amongst a floral carpet of thrift, sea campion or sea mayweed.

Opposite page, top: Puffins rest outside their burrows in a sea of thrift on Lunga, one of the Treshnish Isles, off the Isle of Mull.

Opposite page, bottom: A puffin outside its burrow gazes out to sea from the Westmann Islands.

Above: Puffins on Ingólfshöfði off the south coast of Iceland, which is joined to the mainland by an expanse of notorious quicksands.

Overleaf: A puffin's eye view onto the rocky shore, beneath the spectacular Látrabjarg cliffs in north-west Iceland.

At the beginning of the breeding season, the burrow may need some spring cleaning if the entrance has become partially blocked by the roof collapsing. Where rabbits are present, puffins may take over their shallower burrows because these make for less work than digging out a completely new burrow.

Both birds dig – although the male does the lion's share – using the strong claw-like toes on the webbed feet. The inner claw on each foot is turned inwards so that repeated rock landings do not wear it down. In this way it remains sharp.

Left: After excavating its burrow on a rainy day, a puffin emerges with a muddy chest to stretch its wings.

Above: A pair of puffins emerges from their floriferous burrow entrance on a rainy day on Lunga, Scotland.

Some puffins arrive back at the colony without a mate, either because they have only just reached breeding age or because they have lost a mate in a fishing net or polluted by oil. But even when they manage to pair up they still have to find a nest site.

Early in the season, puffins with existing burrows have to defend their sites while newly paired couples are burrow browsing. It is much less effort to use an old burrow than to dig a new one. Therefore a resident puffin stands guard puffing up its feathers with an open bill in a threat display. If an intruder gets too pushy, puffins can end up fighting with interlocked bills.

In between digging, puffins will pause to court by billing and cooing. One bird approaches the other and begins to swing its bill from side to side. The pair knock their bills broadside with tails raised as they move around on the same spot. Billing also occurs at sea when the puffins rotate in a circle.

If all the existing burrows are occupied, puffins will begin to dig out a new one using their bill as a pickaxe to cut through the turf and also to remove stones. Their feet function as spades or shovels used for digging out the earth from the burrow. Sometimes flying soil will shower the mate standing outside the burrow. Even though puffins take turns to dig, they may not have time to complete a new burrow in one season.

The 70-100cm long burrows are essentially horizontal unless an obstacle – such as an immovable rock – appears in the path. The nest is in a slight hollow at the end of the burrow. A blind side tunnel is also excavated for use as a latrine by the chick. Feathers and plant material are collected in the bill for lining the nest, although the egg often rests on bare rock.

In the northern part of their range, Atlantic puffins will nest in crevices amongst rocky outcrops in northern Norway. Burrowing is impractical in soil that remains frozen until mid-summer at high latitudes.

The density of puffin burrows varies depending on the number of birds and how suitable the area is for burrowing. With six occupied burrows per square metre on Mykines in the Faroe Islands this makes it the most densely populated puffinry.

Opposite page, top left: Excessive burrowing by puffins can lead to erosion as the cliff top slips down into the sea.

Opposite page, top right: Orange encrusting lichens thrive on rocky outcrops where they are fertilised by the seabirds' droppings. Scurvy grass nestles in the rocks here on Grimsey Island, which lies on the Arctic Circle off the north coast of Iceland.

Above left: It is a noisy affair when a pair of puffins knocks their bills together.

Above right: A puffin returns with a beakful of sandeels to feed its chick.

Left: A puffin carries plants in the bill for lining its burrow.

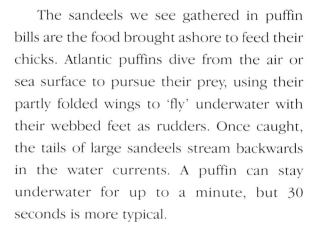

The sandeels we see gathered in puffin bills are the food brought ashore to feed their chicks. Atlantic puffins dive from the air or sea surface to pursue their prey, using their partly folded wings to 'fly' underwater with their webbed feet as rudders. Once caught, the tails of large sandeels stream backwards in the water currents. A puffin can stay underwater for up to a minute, but 30 seconds is more typical.

Auks regularly get caught in gill nets set by Newfoundland fishermen. To discover how deep puffins can dive, fishermen working adjacent to several major seabird colonies in Newfoundland, in the summers of 1980-82, recorded their daily seabird catches along with the depths they fished their nets. Since Atlantic puffins were never found in nets set deeper than 60 metres, it is assumed that this is their maximum diving depth.

Atlantic puffin adults do not restrict their diet to sandeels. They also feed on saithe and whiting, while puffins which breed north of Britain feed on capelin, herring and Arctic cod. In the winter, adult puffins will vary their diet by eating pelagic invertebrates such as polychaete worms, shrimps and molluscs, which they swallow underwater.

It is difficult to determine the range and size of prey taken by non-breeding adult puffins in the open ocean. However, experiments with captive free-swimming puffins and dead fish showed they are capable of swallowing quite large fish, with shallow bodies. Small fish were swallowed underwater, whereas larger fish were brought to the surface to be eaten.

During the non-breeding season, tufted puffins spend most of their time far from land feeding on squid, euphausiids and pelagic fish. The horned puffin is also a pelagic species living in the oceanic waters of the central North Pacific. It too, feeds on squid and other marine invertebrates.

Opposite page, top: Virtually a monoculture of scurvy grass carpets some of the puffin cliffs on Grimsey Island, with bare patches from repeated trampling by puffin feet.

Opposite page, bottom: Sometimes a puffin may return with a single large fish, but a long fish that flaps around as the puffin flies draws attention to food worth hijacking by piratical skuas and other birds.

Right: Euphausiids, such as northern krill (*Meganyctiphanes norvegica*) is one of several planktonic organisms eaten by puffins when they live out at sea during the winter.

Below: A puffin excretes either by walking backwards out of its burrow or by standing on a cliff top and turning its backside towards the sea.

Overleaf: Puffins congregate in clubs on grassy knolls or on flat-topped rocks. Breeding birds gather to relax, while young birds meet up and court potential mates.

Behaviour

Watching the way puffins behave and interact with one another is always a rewarding exercise. Every day, during the breeding season, puffins take off from cliffs to fish and land again on return – making as many as ten round trips a day when feeding their hungry chicks.

Coming into land, a puffin approaches with outstretched wings and spread out legs with the feet lowered like a plane's undercarriage. The actual landing – whether on land or the sea – is often quite clumsy, with the birds crash-landing. On turf-covered land, the puffin quickly recovers, righting itself to adopt a wings up and feet forward posture, so as to appease near neighbours and reduce the likelihood of an attack. If a puffin returns with food, the distance it then walks depends on the contour of the land and whether there is a suitable landing place adjacent to the burrow.

Above: Unlike many seabirds, puffins do not utter raucous calls, and when seen with their bill open this is a threat display to other puffins to keep their distance.

Right: In very windy conditions all the puffins were hunkered down. Then, when an extra strong gust lifted one off the cliff top it hovered hawk-like above the cliff.

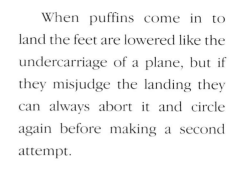

When puffins come in to land the feet are lowered like the undercarriage of a plane, but if they misjudge the landing they can always abort it and circle again before making a second attempt.

Puffins have two quite distinct ways of walking. There is an upright Chaplinesque body walk not unlike that of a penguin; whereas with the head lowered, the profile is reduced as it scurries over the ground towards its burrow before a black-backed gull gets a chance to hijack the catch.

Left: A puffin spreads out its legs and lowers the feet in an attempt to land in a strong wind.

Top left: When puffins walk with an upright body, they strut penguin-like over the ground.

Top right: As well as using their bills to carry fish loads, puffins also use them to preen their feathers. Notice the flexible body allows the puffin to double back to preen the rear of the body.

Left: Once ashore with its fish load, a puffin adopts a quite distinct low rapid shuffling walk – so as to reach its burrow before a gull hijacks the bounty.

Puffins signal ownership of a burrow or space on the ground by stomping up and down on the same spot. As the feet are raised, the red webs are extended to make them more conspicuous.

A puffin takes to the air by pushing off from the ground with both feet that are then held closely together, not unlike a diver taking off from a springboard. Once it is airborne, the short wings normally have to beat fast – as many as 300-400 beats per minute – to keep the stocky body airborne, although upcurrents beside a cliff top will keep a puffin aloft with minimal exercise. Puffins also leave cliffs without frantic flapping, making a graceful flight as they glide down towards the sea. The reason why puffin wings are relatively small is that they are also used for swimming underwater, where large wings would offer too much resistance.

Top: An Atlantic puffin launches itself into the air from a cliff top, with the feet held together and the wings curved inwards.

Middle: In calmer weather, puffins may glide gracefully past cliff tops or over the sea.

Bottom: As puffins dive underwater a stream of air bubbles escapes from beneath their feathers. Note the large toenails project beyond the webbed feet on this tufted puffin.

One of the most memorable aspects of visiting many seabird colonies is the raucous sounds that greet you – notably kittiwakes with their loud 'kitti-waak' calls; puffins however are remarkably unvocal. The loudest noise they make is when a pair knock their bills together, which helps to reinforce the pair-bond. This so-called billing takes place on land as well as on sea. You will also hear loud growling calls beneath your feet, made by puffins in their underground burrows, which can be quite a surprise if you are not expecting them.

Even though puffins will suddenly open their bills as their response to a threat, they do not call out. Fights may occur over possession of a burrow, when beaks become interlocked and growling sounds emerge. During an intense combat the two birds may lose their footing and end up tumbling together down a slope. Whenever a fight takes place, neighbouring puffins gather around looking on with interest. Puffins will also fight on the sea.

Left: Puffins reinforce the pair bond by billing, which is a noisy affair and attracts the attention of a nearby puffin.

In larger or dense colonies – especially where there are predatory gulls or skuas – puffins will adopt a circular wheeling flight. The birds follow a route over the land out to sea and back again, that remains virtually the same from one year to the next. Puffins can join or leave the wheel at any time to move from the sea to their burrows or to leave land for the sea. In a similar way to a fish shoal, a puffin wheel reduces the risk of attack by predators. Whilst in the wheel a puffin can fly past to check for other puffins near its burrow, indicating whether or not it is safe to land. Puffins can also spot a deserted slope – a sign that a predator may be lurking nearby – before deciding whether or not to land the next time round.

At sea, when not submerging to fish, puffins spend much time rafting on the surface, periodically washing or flexing their wings.

Opposite page, top: Tufted puffins in combat on the water surface.

Opposite page, bottom: A tufted puffin snoozes with its bill tucked beneath a wing.

Top: Two Atlantic puffins take a nap by tucking their bills beneath a wing.

Bottom: A tufted puffin washes itself by immersing its body and then flapping its wings. A natural rainbow adds colour to portray the spray as an exploding firework.

Overleaf: Atlantic puffins rafting on the sea surface off Grimsey Island, Iceland.

Reproduction and growing up

Once the burrow has been claimed and cleaned, the female Atlantic puffin can lay her single whitish elliptical egg. If the egg rolls into a crack or an adjacent burrow, or if the pair desert, she will lay another egg two to three weeks later.

Each parent takes turns to incubate the egg, embracing it with a drooping wing beneath one of a pair of bare-skinned brood patches with a copious blood supply. Even when incubating, a puffin may emerge from the burrow for a short spell, safe in the knowledge the egg will be kept warm inside the burrow.

Incubation takes 39-43 days. Hatching begins when the chick uses the egg 'tooth' on the tip of its bill to chip through the shell. The first time a parent comes ashore with a bill full of small fish indicates a chick has hatched. On drying out, the young puffling resembles a dark grey powder puff. It has black legs and feet as well as black bare skin around the eyes. It takes almost a week before the chick is able to maintain its body temperature, so during this time one parent keeps it warm while the other collects food.

Opposite page: Emerging from the dark burrow into bright light outside.

Above: A puffin inspects its burrow on Lunga in Scotland.

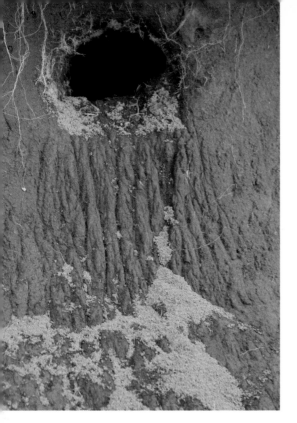

Top left: Where the turf has slumped away on Heimaey, puffins have literally had to claw their way up the vertical earth wall to reach their burrow entrance.

Top right: Once collected, plants are carried back to line the burrow for the chick.

Bottom: A puffin collects grass and other plants by bending down and pulling at the stems with its bill.

Opposite page: The first time an adult returns with a beakful of small fish provides confirmation its chick has just hatched.

Adult puffins collect not only sandeels but also sprats, herring and capelin to feed their hungry youngster; but puffin chicks grow more quickly when fed on oil-rich sandeels. Researchers use mist nets to catch puffins returning with their prey, so that their bill-loads are dropped and the fish can be identified.

The fish are held in the bill by backward-pointing horny papillae on the upper palette and the fleshy tongue. These structures allow a puffin to regularly carry a dozen or more fish crosswise in its bill, with the record standing at 62 fish (61 sandeels and one rockling). Being able to stash many fish in their bill allows puffins to make longer trips to find shoaling fish.

Rarely do puffins bring back a single large fish, because this tends to flap around as the puffin flies, which draws attention for gulls and skuas to dive bomb the puffin in an attempt to persuade it to drop the catch.

Opposite page, top centre: A three-week-old puffin chick is a grey fluff ball with a dark bill. *Photo: Rebecca Nason.*

Opposite page, top right: The secret of how puffins manage to retain many fish within their bills is revealed by a view inside the mouth of a puffin caught by an Icelandic fowler. Both the tongue and the roof of the mouth have backward-pointing horny spines, which prevent the fish from slipping out.

Opposite page, bottom: As the chick grows, larger fish are brought in.

Above: An adult returns with a male snake pipefish with eggs, on Fair Isle in 2006. The chicks find the wiry bodies of these fish difficult to swallow and masses of dead pipefish end up littering the burrows. *Photo: Rebecca Nason.*

The North Sea sandeel stock plummeted after the sandeel fishery caught a million tonnes per year over several decades. As a result, a ban on catching sandeels off the coast of north-east Scotland, south to Northumberland, was introduced in 2000. To help protect this important food for the extensive seabird colonies, the catch limit for the whole North Sea was set to 826,000 tonnes, yet in 2003 the total catch was only 300,000 tonnes.

Rising sea temperatures off Britain in the summers of 2004 and 2005 triggered a northward migration of plankton on which the sandeels feed. The fish also moved north into cooler waters. With their favoured food in short supply, puffins had to find alternative food sources. This period coincided with a population explosion of snake pipefish, which the puffins collected – one at a time – for their chicks. Tragically, not only are these fish much less nutritious prey than sandeels, but also it is difficult for the chicks to swallow such long bony fish. Bird ringers working on the Faroe Islands reported finding many pipefish corpses in the puffin burrows.

The way in which an adult feeds its offspring has been studied by replacing the side of a nest chamber with glass. When the adult returns, it calls to the chick, which emerges from the rear of the burrow and takes a few fish directly from the bill. The rest of the catch is dropped on the floor, from which the chick picks up the fish.

If a chick is brought out into the open from its burrow, it instinctively rushes towards any dark area. This negative response to light ensures the chick stays in its burrow hidden from any bird predators until it is fully fledged. Indeed, if the burrow is too short, so that the puffins incubate in direct light, the chick will not be raised successfully.

The main wing feathers begin to appear after 10-12 days. As the chick increases in size and its appetite increases, the adults cannot afford to linger, so they simply release all the fish, just inside the burrow entrance, before turning around for a repeat trip. The adults spend 34-60 days feeding their chick and by the time it is almost fledged, they are making up to ten round trips per day. When food is in short supply however, the feeding period is prolonged.

Top: A live snake pipefish *(Entelurus aequoreus)* emerging from seaweeds in an aquarium.

Bottom: A ringer on Fair Isle holds a 6-8 week old almost fledged puffin chick. *Photo: Rebecca Nason.*

Top: An immature tufted puffin swims underwater.

Bottom: A year after it hatched at the Living Coasts, an immature tufted puffin has a dull orange bill and drab feet and has yet to develop the splendid golden tufts of the adults.

Once it is fully fledged, the chick leaves the burrow alone at night, when it is least likely to be attacked by predators, and heads for the sea. Most young puffins manage to launch themselves off their cliff top homes for their first flight, ending up splash-landing on the sea below. But on Heimaey, one of the Westmann islands off southern Iceland, some pufflings become disorientated by the lights in the town and end up landing in the streets instead of on the sea. Once they land on the ground, they cannot take off. Fortunately, most of the confused pufflings are rescued by local children, who keep them overnight before releasing them at the coast.

Some pufflings nonetheless fall prey to black-backed gulls and rats in Britain, while arctic foxes and bald eagles feed on tufted puffin chicks in the North Pacific.

Around mid-August, adult puffins leave the breeding grounds around the British coastline and collect together offshore; whereas in Spitzbergen, adults have been observed to provide food for their chicks as late as the last week of September.

Puffins and people

In the past, many small communities, living on remote islands inhabited by breeding seabirds, captured the birds and collected their eggs. Puffin flesh was a valuable fresh food source during the summer months and it was either dried or salted (now deep frozen) for later consumption. In Britain, puffins used to be collected on several islands, including the Isle of Man, Ailsa Craig (with nets placed over burrows at night) and the Isles of Scilly. But the biggest catches were made on St. Kilda off the north west of Scotland, where snares and nooses were used for catching the birds.

Unlike the great auk, puffins are able to escape by flying away if they are not ensnared. Nonetheless, seasoned fowlers are able to catch many birds in a single day.

Opposite page: A puffin displays a threat posture on Látrabjarg cliffs in Iceland.

Above: A puffin flexes its wings after preening.

The main places where Atlantic puffins are still caught are Iceland and the Faroes. They are legally protected during their breeding season in other locations, but can be shot outside the breeding season in Norway from 21 August to 28 February. In the nineteenth century the fowlers on Mykines, one of the Faroe Islands, introduced a large triangular net – not unlike an outsized lacrosse net – on a four-metre-long pole known as a *fleygastong* or simply *fleyg* in English. At this time, as many as a third of a million puffins were caught throughout the Faroe Islands in one season.

Icelanders on Heimaey in the Westmann Islands now also use *fleygs* but here collecting is limited to the period from 1 July to 15 August during the breeding season. Puffins are also shot at sea off Iceland from 1 September to 19 May. On land, the fowlers prefer to work on cool days with light rain, because this is when most birds fly past the cliffs. On warm, sunny days the cliffs are typically deserted, with the puffins out at sea. To avoid collecting breeding birds returning with a fish catch, hunters wait a net's length away from the cliff top edge, where non-breeding birds gather. They often use dead puffins as decoys to lure birds flying past. On a good day, some 200-230 puffins can be caught by a single fowler, but this is half the number caught in 1850 on Ellidaly, another island in the Westmann island group.

Above: A fowler on Heimaey, an island off southern Iceland, carries his huge catch of Atlantic puffins in the 1980s. *Photo: Nordicphotos/Alamy.*

Opposite page: Chilkat dance apron, Tlingit, (1840 – 1850), woven of yarn made from mountain goat wool and cedar bark, mounted on buckskin with fringe trimmed with more than 200 tufted puffin bills. Collected in 1937 from Wrangell, Alaska, by Major Max Fleischmann.
Photo: Steven Timbrook, courtesy Santa Barbara Museum of Natural History.

Fledgling puffins were caught in some parts of Norway using a Norwegian puffin dog or *lundehund* – from *lunde* (puffin) and *hund* (dog). This small dog was specifically bred for puffin hunting to have highly flexible joints, which enables it to squeeze into puffin burrows and pull out live birds. The dog's head can also bend backwards and an extra toe on each foot helps it move over boulder-strewn ground. All parts of the puffin were used; the flesh was eaten and the breast feathers used in place of eiderdown. When other methods were introduced to catch puffins, the *lundehund* almost died out and by the Second World War only six dogs survived. Since then, careful breeding has built up the number of these dogs to about 2000 worldwide.

Tufted puffins were harvested by Inuits along the west coast of North America up to the Aleutians and the Bering Sea. The birds provided fresh meat and some 45 of their cured skins were used to make a single parka lined with puffin breast feathers. Puffin beaks, tied to hoops on hand rattles, were used in ceremonial Chilkat dances. Dance aprons were also decorated with tufted puffin bills, which rattled as the person danced. These beaks were collected both from fresh puffins caught for food, and as bill sheaths shed naturally at the end of the breeding season.

Above: A stray fledged puffling held by a young boy on Heimaey Island in Iceland ready for release. *Photo: Richard T. Nowitz/Corbis.*

Right: A puffin panorama: the Isle of May in the Firth of Forth is one of many seabird islands off Britain where breeding puffins can be seen during a day trip.

Opposite page, bottom: Two tufted puffins chasing each other as they swim on the surface at Living Coasts at Paignton in Devon.

Ironically, the inhabitants of Heimaey Island in Iceland not only slaughter huge numbers of puffins each year, they also help to save many pufflings. When the fledged puffins leave their burrows at night during the latter part of August, some misjudge their exit route and fly towards the street lights, rather than out to sea. Without a helping hand from the Puffin Patrol they would very likely either fall prey to predators or get run over by vehicles. Traditionally, children scour the streets scooping up any errant pufflings, which are taken to the Museum of Natural History to be weighed before being carried home in cardboard boxes and safely released at the coast the next day by throwing them up into the air.

A more positive aspect of the relationship between puffins and people is that wherever a puffin colony is near enough for tourists to make a round trip within a day, local boatmen are assured of a seasonal income. There can be few people who are not instantly captivated by puffins, once seen, creating empathy towards helping to conserve the birds in any way they can.

Not everyone can have the opportunity to experience the thrill of visiting a puffin colony on a remote offshore island during the breeding season. Moreover, for some, the rigours of a small boat trip would be anathema. Yet as more people get to know animals at first hand, the objectives of

conservation become better served. Now there is a new opportunity to experience marine coastal species without exerting greater pressure on wilderness locations.

At the innovative award-winning venture known as Living Coasts in Torquay, Devon, it is possible to see several coastal species – including tufted puffins, fur-seals, gentoo and African penguins – at close quarters. Developed by Paignton Zoo, Living Coasts focuses on the conservation of coastal and marine life from around the globe.

It was opened in 2003, and here you can see some 20 captive-bred tufted puffins moving back and forth from the man-made cliff and the water, and see exactly how they swim below the surface, via a huge underwater viewing area in this sole auk enclosure in Britain. Natural seawater is pumped in from the bay outside and, after circulating through the enclosures and an ozone injected super skimmer, it is ultra violet filtered for 24 hours before being slowly returned to the sea at high tide. To simulate natural conditions around the coast, wave machines generate surges and a tonne of water is dumped in every few minutes. The policy here is to allow the birds to rear their offspring themselves. One tufted puffin chick was produced in 2005 and a year later three chicks were successfully reared.

Top: The underwater viewing area at Living Coasts shows how tufted puffins move on submerging. This bird is carrying green seaweed in its bill.

Above: The large orange bill of the tufted puffin can carry a fish load or nesting material back to the burrow as seen here.

Opposite page: A tufted puffin looks out from its burrow in a man-made cliff at Living Coasts.

Conservation

A variety of factors can cause puffin populations to fluctuate. During the nineteenth century puffins declined as a result of egg collection and the birds being hunted for food. In more recent times, introductions (both accidental and deliberate) of terrestrial predators onto offshore islands have reduced, or even completely wiped out, puffin populations from some islands.

In Britain, rats have been the main problem. For example, in Scotland in the 1870s, there were so many puffins on Ailsa Craig in the Firth of Clyde that when they took to the air, the sky reputedly darkened. But when brown rats arrived on the island – either from shipwrecks or from ships which stopped to deliver coal to the lighthouse – puffin numbers began to decline. By 1930, the tens of thousands of puffins had dwindled to just a few hundred and by the time all the rats were eradicated during the period 1991-92, no puffins had bred on the island for over fifty years. It took a decade for puffins to start breeding again on Ailsa Craig and in 2004 it became an RSPB reserve.

Opposite page: A puffin pauses outside its burrow.

Above: Puffins on Látrabjarg cliffs, Iceland. Over half of the world population of Atlantic puffins breed in this country.

77

Large oil spills present a great threat to seabirds, especially during the breeding season when the birds are concentrated in one area. The 1966 *Sea Empress* spill off Wales occurred in February before puffins had returned to breed; whereas the March 1967 *Torrey Canyon* spill off Cornwall had a devastating effect on French puffins. The Sept Îsles colony off the Brittany coast plummeted from 2500 to 400 pairs, only to be hit by a second spill when the *Amoco Cadiz* super tanker went aground on 16 March 1978 and the colony was further reduced to 200 pairs. The birds were unable to fly at this time because they had lost their primary feathers prior to breeding.

Right: Chocolate-coloured 'mousse' – a mix of seawater, oil and emulsifier – trapped in a steep-sided cove two weeks after the 1996 *Sea Empress* oil spill, fortunately early in the year before the puffins had returned to breed.

Less publicity is given to puffins that get caught up in baited long lines or in gill nets. Yet in 1980, an estimated 7900 puffins – two percent of the local breeding population – were killed, mainly in gill nets, in Witless Bay, Newfoundland. Another hazard for seabirds is the huge amount of pollution in the form of manufactured objects that ends up in the sea. From an examination of stomach contents of dead puffins from the North Sea, one in ten were found to contain pieces of elastic used in clothing. It would appear that puffins mistake these snaking elastic strips for pipefish.

Above: An oiled razorbill drags its wings as it attempts to walk along a beach.

Once puffins have dispersed out at sea, it is virtually impossible to gain an accurate census. The best way is to count the number of occupied burrows during the breeding season. In recent years, natural events have also made an impact on puffin populations in Scotland. Puffins nesting on the east coast have been steadily increasing by some 7 to 12 percent each year. However, this trend was reversed on Craigleith, one of two major puffinries in the Firth of Forth. In just four years, the 1999 population of 28,000 had dwindled to half. During this time there has been a rapid increase of tree mallow, *Lavatera arborea*, a vigorous biennial plant with conspicuous pinkish-purple flowers. This Mediterranean plant is native to south-west and west Britain, but was introduced to seabird islands in the past by lighthouse keepers who used the woolly leaves as a compress for burns.

Top: A rescued oiled puffin being treated at an RSPCA rescue unit.

Bottom: Tree mallow *(Lavatera arborea)* is a vigorous biennial plant that is threatening the puffins on Craigleith, an island in the Firth of Forth. It is growing here on the Lizard in Cornwall.

Initial research by scientists from the Centre for Ecology and Hydrology, seems to suggest that several factors may have brought about this invasion. Milder winters meant this frost-sensitive plant was not kept in check. Tree mallow germinates in open areas and, where puffins excavate their burrows, this encourages germination of tree mallow seedlings. Where there are dense tree mallow stands, the density of puffin burrows markedly decreases; mallow roots make it difficult for puffins to burrow into the soil or gain access to existing burrows.

Also, because the plants can grow up to 2-3 metres tall in their second year, they hide suitable landing spots atop rocks or on open ground for puffins to touch down and make a speedy dash for the safety of their burrows. Longer treks mean that puffins risk attack by gulls. Several possible ways of tackling the tree mallow problem, which has decreased the biodiversity on Craigleith, are under consideration. These include cutting down the plants (digging them up could result in erosion of the burrows); introducing neutered rabbits to keep the mallow in check before the plants get too large; and use of herbicides.

The puffin population on the Isle of May, also in the Firth of Forth, has been extensively studied for over 30 years and here the population has steadily risen, on an island with a healthy rabbit population; apart from 2004 when strong winds and prolonged heavy rain in late June resulted in the death of many puffin chicks within their flooded burrows.

Top: A puffin rests on a rock on Lunga, Scotland.

Climate change has also affected the Atlantic puffins in another way. On land, as spring is getting earlier, so trees begin to leaf out and birds breed earlier. Yet, as North Sea temperatures have increased in recent years, seabirds have been breeding later. This may be because milder winters have delayed the breeding of sandeels, which breed in mid-winter. Also, the food of sandeel larvae – notably the larvae of the northern copepod *Calanus finmarchicus*, is being replaced by a southern species, *C. helgolandicus*, which breeds later. Sandeels are the favoured food for British puffins to feed their chicks. When the North Sea Danish-led sandeel fishery was catching them to produce fishmeal for farm animals and fish farms, it had a dire effect on the breeding success of British seabirds. From 2000, the sandeel fishery was closed along the north-east coast of Scotland to Northumberland and on the Wee Bankie off the Firth of Forth, to safeguard British puffins and kittiwakes which are so dependent on sandeels.

In 2005 and 2006, when sandeel breeding was poor and coincidentally there was a huge increase in snake pipefish, puffins turned to collecting the pipefish to feed their chicks. However, these fish are thin and wiry with little flesh and the chicks have great difficulty in swallowing them. Huge numbers of dead pipefish were found in puffin burrows and those chicks that managed to fledge were underweight.

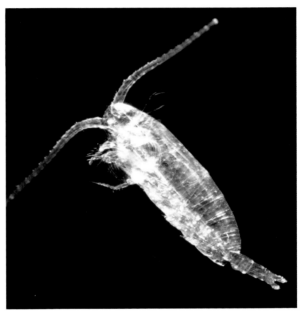

Top: A rabbit emerges from its burrow to graze on a windy day on the Isle of May in the Firth of Forth. Rabbits here keep the vegetation in check and create extensive areas of neat 'lawns'.

Above: *Calanus finmarchicus* is a copepod that forms part of the zooplankton which sandeel larvae favour. Warming sea temperatures are replacing this copepod by a southern species, which breeds later. This can have catastrophic effects on the successful breeding of Atlantic puffins in Scotland.

Within the Gulf of Maine on the east coast of North America, Atlantic Puffins once nested on at least six islands; but persistent hunting for food and feathers, combined with cold summers in the mid 1800s, reduced the population to a single pair south of Canada by the early 1900s. When the lighthouse keepers on Matinicus Rock began to protect the puffins from hunters, their numbers gradually increased to some 210 pairs in 2004. In 1973, the National Audubon Society launched Project Puffin, which aimed to reintroduce puffins to Gulf of Maine islands where they had bred in historic times. Young 10 to14-day-old puffin chicks were brought from Greta Island and fed inside their soil burrows each day for a month.

Puffins imprint on the place where they were reared and since they did not leave Eastern Egg Rock until they were fledged, it was hoped they would recognise this location as their home. During the period 1973–1986, a total of 954 puffin chicks were transferred to Eastern Egg Rock and 914 of these fledged and were ringed. Fortunately all the hard work paid off and in 1977 the first of the transplanted puffins began to return. Wooden puffin decoys and mirrors were placed atop boulders to swell the apparent numbers of puffins and thereby encourage other birds to land. By 2005, there were 72 nesting pairs of puffins in the colony.

Puffin populations have oscillated over the centuries and it is to be hoped they will ride out the new and real threats which climate change is bringing to oceanic food chains in our northern oceans. When breeding sites are lost by turf erosion, puffins seek out alternative sites. Forty-one years after the island of Surtsey was born from the largest submarine eruption near Iceland in recent times, Atlantic puffins began to breed there in two places during the 2004 summer.

Top: Mass of sandeels, for sale in a Guernsey market. Sandeels are long, thin fish that live in large shoals and are the favoured food of the Atlantic puffin.

Opposite page: By facing in opposite directions puffins can be alert all round for danger.

Where to see Atlantic puffins

Iceland

As the Atlantic puffin capital of the world, Iceland is the prime place to see and photograph puffins at many locations on both the main island and smaller offshore islands. Some places are accessible by a short walk from a car, while others require quite a hike after a flight or a boat ride.

From south to north

1   Heimaey, Westmann Islands (S) – access by boat or air.

2   Dyrholaey promontory (SE) near Vik.

3   Ingólfshöfði (SE) – access by 4WD across quicksands.

4   Lundey (Puffin Island) – 3 minutes by boat from Reykjavik.

5   Látrabjarg Cliffs (NW – most westerly place in Europe) – either long drive around the fjords or car ferry from Stykkishólmur to Brjánslækur then drive.

6   Hornbjarg and Hornstrandir in Natural Reserve Park (W).

7   Grimsey Island (N of Iceland on arctic circle at 66°33'N) – access by boat or air.

Please note: maps are not drawn to scale.

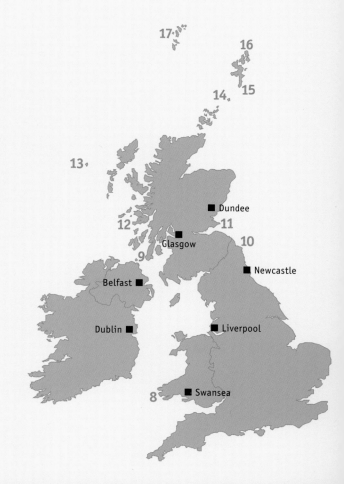

Great Britain

From south to north

8   Skokholm and Skomer Islands, Wales – access by boat.

9   Rathlin Island Cliffs, Co Antrim, Northern Ireland – access by boat.

10 Farne Islands, Northumberland – access by boat.

11 Isle of May NNR, Firth of Forth – access by boat.

12 Isle of Lunga, Treshnish Isles, off Mull – access by boat.

13 St. Kilda – access by boat.

14 Fair Isle – access by air.

15 Shetland Isles – Sumburgh Head, Noss NNR.

16 Hermaness NNR – access by boat or air.

Faroe Islands, Denmark

17 Mikines.

Norway

18 Røst

North America

19 Maine Coastal Islands National Wildlife Refuge (NWR), Maine.

20 Witless Bay, Newfoundland, Canada.

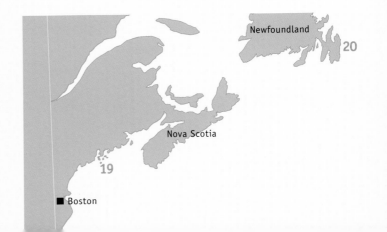

Photo tips and hints

With their colourful and comical faces it is not surprising that photogenic puffins rank high on the list of most popular birds to photograph. However, the pioneer British wildlife photographer, Richard Kearton, was far from enthusiastic about this seabird when he wrote in his book, *With Nature and a Camera* (1898): "A puffin is a grotesque-looking bird at any time during the breeding season…".

Puffins are accessible for only a few months during their breeding season. The best locations tend to be offshore islands on which it may be impossible to land during rough weather.

Right: In poor light, a slow shutter speed produces a more creative impression of a puffin leaping from a cliff on Grimsey Island, Iceland.

A variety of lenses can be used, from a wide angle (to show puffins in their habitat), a medium length zoom (such as 100-300mm) to a long focus 500mm. Many shots in this book were taken with my favourite 200-400mm VR lens. With care and patience, it is possible to get remarkably close to some puffins, but they tend to be more wary of people in places where the birds are captured for food. However, their small size means that a long telephoto lens will ensure frame-filling portraits without any risk of disturbing the birds. Getting too close not only means puffins will use up energy fleeing from the cliff tops (which delays chicks being fed), but also you will fail to get your pictures.

Approach slowly, reducing your profile by crawling forward on all fours and, if need be, finally lying down and inching forward by wriggling on your tummy. A better perspective is gained by working at the puffins' level instead of looking down on them from above. I like to sit down and set up a tripod fairly close to the ground, taking care not to collapse the roofs of cliff top burrows by getting too close.

Sometimes on arrival at a puffin colony, it appears completely deserted when all the adults are out at sea fishing. But if you sit down patiently, they will return. Most puffins will be seen outside their burrows at the end of the day. I have photographed puffins in all weathers – in sun, fog and rain and when a strong wind was blowing. Providing the camera equipment is well protected with a waterproof camera cover (or a plastic bag securely sealed with an elastic band around the lens) it is possible to keep shooting in the rain.

With the exception of some images that have been cropped, all photographs in this book appear as they were taken.

Opposite page: Keeping a low profile to photograph puffins in Iceland.

Above: Rimlit by the late evening sun, an Atlantic puffin returns to the Isle of May with a sandeel catch.

Puffin names

The origin of a name is always intriguing and puffin in various languages is no exception. Puffin possibly derives from the Old English *pyffan* to puff out, and from the Middle English *puffen* to puff. Both the Dutch *(Papegaaiduiker)* and German *(Papageitaucher)* names for puffin mean parrot-diver.

The names for puffin in various Scandinavian languages share a common derivation: Icelandic – *Lundi*; Faroese – *Lundin*; Shetlandic – *Londi*; Norwegian – *Lunde* and Swedish – *Lunnefågel*. This is possibly from the Old Norse word *lundi*, referring to the lines or veins in a piece of cut wood or stone; or in this case, to the markings on the puffin's beak.

Lying off the north Devon coast in the Bristol Channel is Lundy Island, so-named from the Norse *lund-ey*, meaning Puffin Island. Sadly, the puffin population on this island plummeted from more than 3,500 pairs in 1939 to less than 10 pairs in 2000. Their demise was due to the island's rat population – originating from a few animals that crawled ashore from shipwrecks some 200 years ago – which feasted on both puffin eggs and chicks. Starting in 2003, it took two years to eradicate all the Lundy rats by laying poisoned bait and it is now hoped that the puffins will gradually be able to rebuild their numbers on this, their island.

Information and Acknowledgements

Information

Internet sites

More information about puffins can be found on the following internet sites.

National Audubon Society
Project Puffin
http://www.projectpuffin.org/what.html

Puffin cams

Isle of May NNR, Firth of Forth, Scotland
A webcam switches between two cameras on an island where some 100,000 puffins and other seabirds breed.
http://www.seabird.org/web-cam.asp

Living Coasts, Devon
This site has a tufted puffin cam looking into a burrow switched on when the puffins are breeding.
http://www.livingcoasts.org.uk

Skomer Island, Wales
Two webcams will be live on Skomer during 2007 – at The Wick and North Haven – which can be accessed via the website below.
http://www.welshwildlife.org

Seal Island NWR, Maine, USA
The camera shows a puffin roosting ledge with wooden puffin decoys used to attract puffins and rotates to show the nesting habitat beneath granite boulders.
http://www.audubon.org/bird/puffin/puffin-cam.html

Above: A rear view of a puffin flying from a cliff top in windy conditions.

94

Acknowledgements

Many people helped in the production of this book. I should especially like to thank Lucy Simpson who did a superb job researching and also proof-reading the entire book. Professor Rory McTurk for providing information on the names for puffins in various Scandinavian languages as well as the etymology of *Lundi*. Kate Carter assisted with inputting copy and proof-reading. The photos are a mixture of transparencies (all meticulously scanned by Justin Harrison) and original digital files. The Living Coasts made me most welcome at their award-winning coastal exhibit in Devon.

Bibliography

Roy Dennis, 1990, *Puffins*. Colin Baxter Photography, Lanark, Scotland.

Errol Fuller, 2003, *The Great Auk – The Extinction of the Original Penguin*. Bunker Hill Publishing, Boston, USA.

M.P. Harris, 1984, *The Puffin*. T & A.D. Poyser, Calton, England.

Bruce McMillan, 1995, *Nights of the Pufflings*. Houghton Mifflin Company, Boston, USA.

Kenny Taylor, 2001, *Puffins*. Colin Baxter Photography, Grantown-on-Spey, Scotland.

Other Wildlife Monographs titles published by

Evans Mitchell Books

Wildlife Monographs
Brown Bears
ISBN: 978-1-901268-50-8

Wildlife Monographs
Humpback Whales
ISBN: 978-1-901268-56-0

Wildlife Monographs
Giant Pandas
ISBN: 978-1-901268-13-3

Wildlife Monographs
Monkeys of the Amazon
ISBN: 978-1-901268-10-2

Wildlife Monographs
Polar Bears
ISBN: 978-1-901268-15-7

Wildlife Monographs
Cheetahs
ISBN: 978-1-901268-09-6

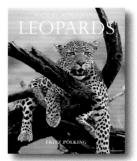

Wildlife Monographs
Loepards
ISBN: 978-1-901268-12-6

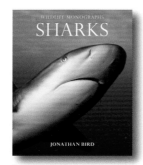

Wildlife Monographs
Sharks
ISBN: 978-1-901268-11-9

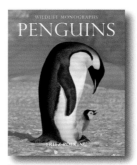

Wildlife Monographs
Penguins
ISBN: 978-1-901268-14-0

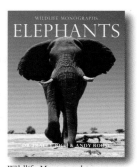

Wildlife Monographs
Elephants
ISBN: 978-1-901268-08-9

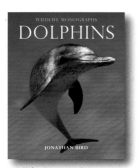

Wildlife Monographs
Dolphins
ISBN: 978-1-901268-17-1

Wildlife Monographs
Wolves
ISBN: 978-1-901268-18-8

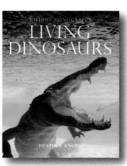

Wildlife Monographs
Living Dinosaurs
ISBN: 978-1-901268-36-2

Wildlife Monographs
Snow Monkeys
ISBN: 978-1-901268-37-9